To Marc, who sees the poetry in hayfields,
and to Erica for sharing her haymaking reflections.

Thanks to my friends, neighbors, and partners in haying:
Anne, Gus, Marianne, and Richard.
—C. M.

For Rosa María and Adrienne, mother and daughter.
—J. C.

Library of Congress Cataloging-in-Publication Data
Names: Mihaly, Christy, author. | Cepeda, Joe, illustrator.
Title: Hey, hey, hay! / by Christy Mihaly ; illustrated by Joe Cepeda.
Description: First edition. | New York : Holiday House, [2018]
Identifiers: LCCN 2017000824 | ISBN 9780823436668 (hardcover)
Subjects: LCSH: Hay—Juvenile literature. | Hay—Harvesting—Juvenile literature.
Classification: LCC SB198 .M55 2018 | DDC 633.2—dc23 LC record available at https://lccn.loc.gov/2017000824

HEY, HEY, HAY!

A Tale of Bales and the Machines That Make Them

by
Christy Mihaly

illustrated by
Joe Cepeda

Holiday House **New York**

On a cold and wintry day,
I love to break out bales of hay.

The hay smells fresh, like summer sun.
I feed my horses, one by one.

Listen, and I'll tell the tale
of storing summer in a bale.

Every June, when grass turns green,
our hayfield makes a pretty scene.

When it's high enough, we mow.
On cutting day, we're set to go!

Mower blades slice through the grass.
A new row falls with every pass.

Stalks and stems are scattered 'round.
The scents of new-mown plants abound.

Next we run the tedder through
to fluff the grass and dry the dew.

Underneath the sun's bright rays,
we feel the heat of summer's blaze.

Mom calls out, "Let's take a break . . .

for switchel and a piece of cake!"

Hay must dry for several days
beneath the summer sun's warm rays.

Once it's had a chance to dry,
we rake the windrows long and high.

"Baling time," I hear Mom shout.
It's time to drive the baler out.

Up and down the windrow trails,
that baler rolls hay into bales.

We gather up the bales and then . . .

we store them in our barn again.

This year's crop is stashed away
and ready for a winter's day.

Mower, tedder, baler—hay!
We're haying on a summer day.

Hey, hey, hay!

Haymaking Words

Bale: a bundle of hay, which may be round or square.

Baler: a machine that rolls or packs the loose, dried hay into neat packages for storage.

Hay: grass, clover, alfalfa, and similar green plants that have been cut and dried, to be used to feed animals such as horses, cows, sheep, and goats.

Hay rake: a tool that gathers cut hay into long windrows.

Mower: a machine that cuts grass. The farm mower is an extra-large lawn mower.

Switchel: a drink, sometimes called "haymakers' punch," traditionally made for thirsty workers at haying time.

Tedder: a machine that picks up and spreads cut hay so it dries quickly and evenly.

Tractor: a strong, big-wheeled vehicle used on farms to pull attachments (mowers, tedders, rakes, balers, etc.) and to lift and move things (like hay bales).

Windrows: long piles of hay in the field, ready to be baled.

Make Your Own Switchel

INGREDIENTS:

2 tablespoons apple cider vinegar

4 tablespoons pure maple syrup

1 teaspoon fresh grated ginger

4 cups water

Combine the ingredients in a large jar with a lid and shake. Pour the mixture over ice cubes to serve right away, or chill it in the refrigerator for a few hours. Stir well before pouring it into your glass. Makes about a quart.